A Book of Dog Breeds for Children:
They're All Dogs

By Amber Richards

There are many different kinds of dogs, called dog breeds. Even when they look very different from each other, they are all dogs.

Great Dane

This dog breed is called a Great Dane. They are very big dogs. Some Great Danes can be bigger than small ponies. They have a bark that is low, slow and very deep. They say, "Woof, woof" loudly. Can you bark like a Great Dane?

Irish Wolfhound

This dog breed is an Irish Wolfhound. They are very big dogs too; in fact, they are the tallest dogs of all dog breeds.

Chihuahua

This dog breed is called a
Chihuahua. They are one of the
smallest dogs. No matter how
much they eat, or how old they
get, they will never grow very big.
They have a tiny, high and fast
bark that sounds like, "yip, yip,
yip." Can you bark like a
Chihuahua?

Poodle

This dog breed is called a poodle. Poodles have very curly hair, and sometimes they have very different haircuts. Some poodles are very small, and some are big, and they come in many different colors.

Afghan Hound

This dog breed is an Afghan Hound. They have very long hair and a curly tail. They can run very fast.

Chinese Crested Dog

This dog breed is a Chinese Crested dog. It mostly has no hair, except some long hair on their heads and tails. Even though these dogs look different and have no fur, they are still dogs too. What kind of a bark do you think these dogs have?

Dalmatian

This dog breed is called a
Dalmatian. Is it a white dog with
black spots, or a black dog with
white spots? These are good
dogs for firemen, and some even
live at the firehouse.

Golden Retriever

This dog breed is a Golden Retriever. They are medium sized dogs and they love to play, swim in water, and catch a ball. Their bark is a happy, "ruff, ruff." Can you bark like a Golden Retriever?

Shar Pei

This breed of dog is called a Shar Pei. No other kind of dog looks like them, they have super wrinkly skin. Sometimes the skin will even fall over the eyes when they move.

Dachshund

The Dachshund breed of dog is sometimes called a wiener dog, because it's very long body is shaped like a hotdog. They have very short legs, so they run slowly.

Puli

This breed of dog is called a Puli.
It's usually black and has long,
rope like curls for its fur. They
like to chase and herd sheep.

Labrador Retrievers

This dog breed is a Labrador Retriever, or a lab for short. They are usually black, golden or brown. They love water and swimming and are loyal friends.

Pomeranian

This breed of dog is called a Pomeranian. It is a small dog with lots of fluffy fur; in fact sometimes people call it a pom-pom.

Brussels Griffon

This dog breed is called a Brussels Griffon, they are small dogs with very cute faces. They like to howl. Can you make a tiny howl like a Brussels Griffon?

English Bulldog

This breed of dog is called the English Bulldog. They are short dogs with flat noses. Because they have flat noses, sometimes they snort when they breathe or get excited. Sometimes they look like they are pouting. Can you snort like a bulldog?

Basenji

This breed of dog is called a Basenji. It's a small dog with a curly tail. What's different about this dog is that it doesn't bark. It does however; make a strange noise called a yodel, a hoarse squeak sound that is quiet. Can you try to make the sound you think it might make?

Greyhound

This dog breed is called a Greyhound. They are very thin dogs and sometimes race, because they are very fast runners.

Alaskan Malamute

The Alaskan Malamute dog breed
has thick heavy fur to keep them
warm in very cold weather.
These dogs pull special sleds
through deep snow, for people to
ride on.

American Boxer

The American boxer is a popular family pet. They love to run, jump and play and can be rowdy when they are young. Sometimes they snort. Can you snort like a boxer?

Bloodhound Dog

Bloodhound dogs sometimes look like they have sad eyes. They have a great sense of smell and many times are working dogs because of that. They have a deep, bark that is long and sometimes almost sounds like there's a little cough. Can you try it the sound?

St. Bernard

St. Bernard dogs are very large, loyal dogs. Sometimes they are used to help rescue people who are lost, which is why you see them with a keg. They can snore loudly when they sleep.

There are many other dog breeds too. You can see some dogs are big, small, strange or silly looking, curly hair, no hair, long hair, short hair, polka dotted and in all colors, but they are all still dogs.

Watch out to see what kinds of dogs you can find.
The end.

If you have enjoyed this book in any way, would you consider leaving a review on Amazon? It is greatly appreciated!

Made in the USA
Lexington, KY
27 January 2016